博古通今

Gems of the Chinese Language Through the Ages

谚语 100

100 Pearls of Chinese Wisdom

尹斌庸　编著

韩　晖　翻译

田　园　绘图

华语教学出版社

SINOLINGUA

First Edition   1999
Second Printing 2000
Third Printing   2001

ISBN 7-80052-709-3
Copyright 1999 by Sinolingua
Published by Sinolingua
24 Baiwanzhuang Road, Beijing 100037, China
Tel: 86-10-68326333/68996153
Fax:86-10-68994599
E-mail: sinolingua@ihw.com.cn

Printed by Beijing Foreign Languages Printing House
Distributed by China International
Book Trading Corporation
35 Chegongzhuang Xilu, P.O.Box 399
Beijing 100044, China

Printed in the People's Republic of China

前　言

　　学习汉语的外国学生，当他们初步掌握了汉语的语音、词汇、语法和文字时，很想进一步提高自己的汉语水平。怎样提高呢?一件重要的事就是需要掌握一些汉语语言中最有特色的东西——例如典故、成语、谚语、歇后语。这些东西既和汉语汉字有密切关系，又和汉族的文化背景有密切关系。掌握了它们，不但能够丰富外国人汉语的表达能力，而且也能够增强他们汉语表达的民族特色。简而言之,他们所掌握的汉语就更像汉语了。这就为成为一个"中国通"迈出了重要的一步。

　　为以上目的，我们给这样的外国学生编了一套"博古通今学汉语丛书"，包括"典故 100"、"成语 100"、"谚语 100"和"歇后语 100"。

　　本套书精选汉语中最有价值的、常用的、表现力强的成语、谚语、歇后语、典故各 100 则。每则均附英文释义，每则配一幅精美插图，另有一些难解词语中英文注释。

Preface

What is the next step for a foreign student of the Chinese language after mastering the phonetics, grammar, and a fair amount of vocabulary? It is highly desirable to grasp something typical Chinese—like idioms, set phrases, proverbs or even the two-part allegorical sayings peculiar to Chinese. These idioms are so closely related to Chinese culture that once one has mastered them, one will not only be able to speak idiomatic Chinese and sound more like a native speaker, but also penetrate deeper into Chinese culture, and gradually become a "China Hand".

For this purpose, we have composed this *Gems of the Chinese Language Through the Ages* series, which comprises the following four books:

The Stories Behind 100 Chinese Idioms
100 Pearls of Chinese Wisdom
100 Common Chinese Idioms and Set Phrases
100 Chinese Two-Part Allegorical Sayings

These idioms and proverbs have been chosen for their frequency of use, practical value and expressiveness.

Each one is accompanied by an English translation and an appropriate illustration. Some obscure expressions are clarified with the help of annotations in both Chinese and English.

目　　录
Contents

attention; one word may be worth a thousand pieces of gold.

If you work hard enough at it, you can grind even
an iron rod down to a needle.

As a man sows, so shall he reap.

八字衙门朝南开，有理无钱莫进来

bāzì yámen cháo nán kāi, yǒu lǐ wú qián mò jìnlái

The *yamen* gate is wide open, yet with only right on your side but no money, don't go inside.

衙门的大门朝南开着，有理却没有钱的人别想进去告状。

这条谚语告诉我们：过去官府腐败，只贪图老百姓的钱财，而不为老百姓办事。

This proverb, dating from feudal times, warns the unwary not to seek justice from the corrupt and greedy officials of those days.

衙门：是旧时官员办公审案的地方。衙门的两扇大门开
　　　着像个"八"字。
　　　Government office in old feudal China. 八字 here
　　　refers to the shape of the open gate.

兵马未动，粮草先行

bīngmǎ wèi dòng, liángcǎo xiān xíng

Provisions should be arranged before an army is mobilized.

作战的部队还没有动身，军用的粮草就先运足了。

这条谚语告诉我们：无论是打仗或做任何一件工作，都必须事先做好充分物质准备，才能有成功的把握。

This proverb stresses that whatever we do, proper preparations should be made in advance to ensure success.

兵马：兵士和战马,泛指作战部队。
　　Soldiers and horses; generally, an army.
粮草：军用的粮食和草料。
　　Food and fodder provided for an army.

不经一事，不长一智

bù jīng yī shì, bù zhǎng yī zhì

Wisdom comes from experience.

不亲身经历一件事情，就不能增长对这方面的见识。

这条谚语告诉我们：要想对一件事情有深刻的了解，最重要的是亲自去实践、体验一下。

This proverb tells us that experience or practice is the best way to learn something.

智：智慧、见识。

Wisdom, knowledge.

不入虎穴，焉得虎子？

bù rù hǔxué, yān dé hǔzǐ?

How can you catch tiger cubs without entering the tiger's lair?

　　不进入老虎住的山洞，怎么能够得到老虎崽儿呢？

　　这条谚语告诉我们：只有勇于探索，不畏风险，才能取得成功。

This proverb tells us that one cannot expect to achieve success without experiencing difficulties and risks; only those who are bold in exploring and not afraid of hardships and dangers can achieve success.

穴：岩洞、山洞。

　　Cave, den.

焉：是疑问代词"怎么"的意思。

　　An interrogative pronoun meaning "how?".

焉得：怎么能得到。

　　How can you obtain. . . ?

差之毫厘，失之千里

chà zhī háo lí, shī zhī qiān lǐ

A little error may lead to a large discrepancy.

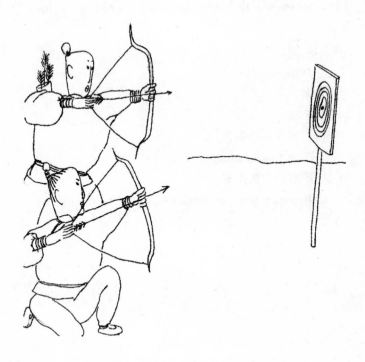

开始时只稍微差了一点点，结果会造成很大的失误。

这条谚语告诉我们：做事情要力求细心、准确，哪怕是极微小的差错，也容易造成非常大的损失。

This proverb advises that when doing something one must make every effort to be careful and exact, because even a tiny mistake can lead to a great loss.

差：不相同。

　　Difference.

失：失误。

　　Fault.

毫厘：形容非常小的数量。

　　Very tiny in amount.

千里：形容很大的距离。

　　Referring to a long distance.

长江后浪催前浪，世上新人赶旧人

Cháng Jiāng hòu làng cuī qián làng, shì shàng xīn rén gǎn jiù rén

Just as the waves of the Yangtze River behind drive on those ahead, so does each new generation replace the old one.

　　长江里，后面的浪花推动着前面的浪花；世界上，新一代的人追赶着老一代的人。

　　这条谚语告诉我们：社会在不断进步，事物在不断发展，新的代替旧的是不可抗拒的客观规律。

This proverb spells out the irresistible objective law that the new continuously replaces the old.

常将有日思无日，莫待无时想有时

cháng jiāng yǒu rì sī wú rì, mò dài wú shí xiǎng yǒu shí

When rich, think of poverty, but don't think of riches when you are poor.

　　富裕的时候，要常常想到可能有贫穷的那一天；不要等到贫穷了，再来回忆富裕时的生活。

　　这条谚语告诉我们：勤俭节约是管理家庭、治理国家的根本方针。富日子要当穷日子过，不要等到钱花光了才后悔。

This proverb indicates that frugality is the best policy: Be frugal even when you are rich, and don't dream of riches when you are poor, but work hard and be thrifty.

将：把。

　　The same as 把.

待：等到。

　　To wait.

吃一堑，长一智

chī yī qiàn, zhǎng yī zhì

A fall into the pit, a gain in your wit.

这条谚语告诉我们：一个人受到一次挫折以后，如果能够总结经验教训，就能增长见识和智慧。

This proverb's message is: Having gone through a setback, one will have gained experience and wisdom, which will be useful if only one can take warning and learn something from the setback.

吃：在这里有遭受、经受的意思。

Here 吃 means to suffer, to experience.

堑（qiàn）：是隔断交通的沟，引申为挫折。

A ditch which cuts off traffic; here, by extension, it means a setback.

打蛇不死，后患无穷

dǎ shé bù sǐ, hòuhuàn wúqióng

Unless you beat a snake to death, it will cause endless trouble in future.

打蛇如果不彻底打死，就会带来无穷无尽的祸患。

这条谚语告诉我们：消灭恶势力如果不彻底，恶势力总有一天会更加猖狂地反扑过来，造成无穷无尽的灾难。

This proverb warns us that: If evil is not eliminated completely, it will not rest until it has destroyed us.

后患：以后的祸患。
　Future trouble, disastrous aftermaths.
穷：尽头。
　End.

大处着眼，小处着手

dà chù zhuóyǎn, xiǎo chù zhuóshǒu

Keep the general goal in sight while tackling daily tasks.

从大的地方认真观察、考虑，从小的地方开始动手干起来。

这条谚语告诉我们：办一件事情，一方面要从全局考虑，看得远些；另一方面又要扎扎实实地从点滴做起。

This proverb advises us to always keep the overall situation in mind and be far-sighted while we set our hands to mundane business.

处：地方。

　　Place.

着眼：观察、考虑。

　　To observe, consider.

着手：开始做。

　　To undertake.

单丝不成线，独木不成林

dānsī bù chéng xiàn, dúmù bù chéng lín

A single thread can't make a cord, nor a single tree a forest.

一根丝搓不成线，一棵树木构不成森林。

这条谚语告诉我们：一个人的力量是有限的，不能做成大事情。只有依靠集体的力量，才能干成大事业。

This proverb tells us that the power of one person is limited. Only when everybody pulls together, can they achieve their goals.

当局者迷，旁观者清

dāngjú zhě mí, pángguān zhě qīng

The spectators see more of the game than the players.

　　拿着棋子下棋的人往往容易迷惑糊涂，在旁边观看下棋的人反而常常看得更加清楚。

　　这条谚语告诉我们：一件事情的当事人，往往因为对利害得失考虑太多，看问题反而不全面；而局外人常常能够冷静地观察思考，所以反而看得更加清楚。

This proverb points out that a person involved in a matter usually does not have a comprehensive overview of it due to too much concentration on gains and losses, while the onlookers, who have a calmer and more objective attitude, have a better grasp of what is going on.

当局者：原指下棋的人。
　　Originally referring to the player.
旁观者：指在旁边观看的人。
　　The spectators.

刀不磨要生锈，水不流要发臭

dāo bù mó yào shēngxiù, shuǐ bù liú yào fāchòu

A knife will rust if not sharpened regularly, and water will stagnate if it is not allowed to flow.

刀要经常磨，不磨就容易生锈；水要不断流，不流就容易发臭。

这条谚语告诉我们：人要不断学习，不断进取，否则就会落后，甚至变坏。身体也要经常活动锻炼，否则就会生病。

This proverb denotes that one has to keep studying to avoid falling behind or even degenerating, and to keep doing physical exercises to prevent sickness.

道高一尺，魔高一丈

dào gāo yī chǐ, mó gāo yī zhàng

The law is strong, but the outlaws are ten times stronger.

道行增高一尺,魔怪跟着增高一丈。

这条谚语来源于佛教,用来告诫修行的人,道行的增高很不容易, 而受到魔怪的诱惑丧失道行却很容易。引申的意思是:成为一个好人需要经过长时期的努力,变成一个坏人却非常的快。

This proverb comes from Buddhism. It stresses that it is difficult to achieve goodness, which is easy to lose when the devil tempts us. The extended meaning is that one needs a long period of strenuous effort to become a good man, but one can easily learn to be a bad one.

道行:僧道修行的功夫。

The attainments of a Taoist priest.

灯不拨不亮，理不辩不明

dēng bù bō bù liàng, lǐ bù biàn bù míng

An oil lamp becomes brighter after trimming, a truth becomes clearer after being discussed.

油灯不时常拨动就不明亮，道理不经过辩论就不能分清是非。过去用的油灯，燃烧一段时间后，需要把灯芯上烧成灰烬的灯花拨掉，灯光才会重新明亮。

这条谚语告诉我们：对于一个复杂的问题，只有通过不同意见的讨论和争论，最后才能弄明白，得出正确的结论。

In the past, after an oil lamp had burned for some time it had to be trimmed, otherwise the light would grow dimmer.

This proverb tells us that facing a complicated problem, only by discussion and debate can we get the correct answer. Truth develops through the comparison of ideas.

读书须用意，一字值千金

dú shū xū yòng yì, yī zì zhí qiān jīn

When reading, don't let a single word escape your attention; one word may be worth a thousand pieces of gold.

读书的时候必须专心一意，不要放过每一个字，有的字非常重要，真是可以说价值千金。

这条谚语告诉我们：学习要专心致志，弄懂弄通每一个字词。只有这样读书，才能够有所收获。

This proverb stresses the fact that study requires undivided attention. No single word should be passed over before we fully understand it. Only in this way can study be rewarded.

用意：专心一意。

Whole hearted.

读万卷书，行万里路

dú wàn juàn shū, xíng wàn lǐ lù

Read ten thousand books and walk ten thousand miles.

要增长知识,就要读很多很多的书;要开阔眼界,就要走很多很多的路。

这条谚语告诉我们:读书可以增加间接知识,观察可以增加直接知识。一个人要读很多的书,才能够做到知识广博;要走许多路,才能丰富自己的见闻。两者都不可缺少。

This proverb tells us that reading will enlarge one's second-hand knowledge, while observing will enrich one's first-hand knowledge. Both are indispensable for one to achieve true wisdom.

万卷书:形容书很多。
　　A lot of books.
万里路:形容路很长。
　　A long distance.

儿不嫌母丑，狗不嫌家贫

ér bù xián mǔ chǒu, gǒu bù xián jiā pín

A son never thinks his mother ugly, and a dog never shuns its owner's home however shabby it is.

儿子从来不会嫌弃养育自己的母亲长得丑陋，忠实的狗永远不会嫌弃自己的主人家里贫穷。

这条谚语告诉我们：与自己息息相关的亲人，即使有一些不足的地方，也不会嫌弃他们的。照此类推，对于自己的家乡和祖国，即使还存在一些不足的地方，我们也永远不会嫌弃她们的。

This proverb reminds us never to despise those nearest and dearest to us, no matter how plain and insignificant they are.

儿孙自有儿孙福，莫为儿孙做马牛

érsūn zì yǒu érsūn fú, mò wèi érsūn zuò mǎniú

The children can take care of themselves when they grow up, so the parents don't have to work too hard for the future of their offspring.

子孙后代各人有自己的福分，不必为他们做牛做马。

这条谚语告诉我们：应该正确对待子孙后代的前途问题。子孙后代各人有自己的生活道路，家长过分地为他们忧虑、操劳是多余的。

This proverb tells us that the older generation should take a proper attitude toward the future of the younger generation. It is not necessary for parents to worry too much about their children, since they will make their own way in the world.

福：福分，享受幸福生活的命运。

Good luck, a happy lot.

耳听为虚，眼见为实

ěr tīng wéi xū, yǎn jiàn wéi shí

What you hear about may be false, but what you see is true.

只凭耳朵听容易得到虚假的东西，只有亲眼见到才是切实可靠的。

这条谚语告诉我们：传闻常常是不可靠的，亲自观察才能了解事情的真相。不能听信谣言，要以事实为根据。

This proverb cautions that: Hearsay is generally unreliable. The truth can not be obtained without close observation. Rumor should not be believed and facts speak loudest of all.

虚:虚假。
  False.
实:真实。
  Truth.

凡人不可貌相，海水不可斗量

fán rén bù kě màoxiàng, hǎishuǐ bù kě dǒu liáng

As a man cannot be known by his looks, neither can the sea be fathomed by a gourd.

一个人不可凭外貌来判断他怎么样，海里的水不能用斗来进行度量。

这条谚语告诉我们：不能光凭外表来评价一个人，这样做常常会犯很大的错误。

This proverb notes that judging by appearance may lead to serious mistakes.

凡:凡是。

　　Any.

貌:相貌。

　　Appearance.

相:动词,看外表来判断优劣。貌相,可以颠倒词序来理解,即看相貌,看外表。

　　(Here a verb) to judge by appearance; 貌相 can be understood by transposing the order of the two words.

斗:是过去用来量粮食的器具。

　　A gourd dipper used to measure grains in olden times.

放下屠刀，立地成佛

fàngxià túdāo, lìdì chéng fó

The butcher who lays down his knife, at once becomes a Buddha.

放下屠宰牲畜的刀子再不干了，立刻就能成为修行圆满的人了。

这条谚语告诉我们：即使是作恶多端的人，只要诚心悔改，从此以后再不干坏事，就可以成为一个好人。

This proverb tells us that even an evildoer can become a good person as long as he sincerely repents and earnestly reforms himself.

立地：立刻。

　　At once.

佛：佛教徒称修行圆满的人。

　　Buddha, a saintly person.

风无常顺，兵无常胜

fēng wú cháng shùn, bīng wú cháng shèng

A boat can't always sail with the wind; an army can't always win battles.

行船不可能每次都遇到顺风，打仗也不可能每次都得胜利。

这条谚语告诉我们：做任何事情都不可能一帆风顺，总是会遇到一些困难或挫折。我们对于困难和挫折，必须有充分的思想准备。

This proverb urges us to be fully prepared for difficulties and setbacks: It is impossible to have smooth sailing all the time.

常:经常。

Always.

兵:军队。

Troops.

逢人只说三分话, 未可全抛一片心

féng rén zhǐ shuō sān fēn huà, wèi kě quán pāo yī piàn xīn

Talking to a stranger, it is wise to be somewhat reserved.

对一般的人，说话只宜讲三分留七分，千万不要把心里话全抛了出去。

这条谚语告诉我们：社会上太复杂，什么样的人都有。轻易相信别人，常常容易上当。所以说话应当谨慎、留有余地。

This proverb cautions us to be careful not to reveal our inner thoughts to a person before we know him or her properly. Being incautious, one is liable to be cheated.

瓜无滚圆, 人无十全

guā wú gǔnyuán, rén wú shí quán

No melon is completely round, and no person is perfect.

瓜找不到一个非常非常圆的，人找不到一个非常非常完美的。

这条谚语告诉我们：任何人都不可能十全十美，也就是说，不可能要求一个人没有一点缺点。

This proverb reminds us not to demand perfection.

滚圆：就是非常圆。

Completely round.

十全：完美无缺。

Perfect.

害人之心不可有,防人之心不可无

hài rén zhī xīn bù kě yǒu, fáng rén zhī xīn bù kě wú

One shouldn' t have the heart to harm others, but must be vigilant so as not to be harmed.

伤害别人的想法不应该有，防备别人的想法却不可以没有。

这条谚语告诉我们：坏人总是有的，时时处处提高警惕非常必要。我们不伤害任何人，但也不要让任何人伤害我们。

This proverb counsels us to be vigilant at all times. Don't do harm to others, but don't allow others to do harm to you.

花有重开日，人无再少年

huā yǒu chóng kāi rì, rén wú zài shàonián

Flowers may bloom again, but a person never has the chance to be young again.

花儿谢了，还能有重新开放的那一天；人的少年时代过去了，以后再也不会回来。

这条谚语告诉我们：青春年华一去永不复返，要珍惜好年华，不要荒废青春啊!

This proverb warns us that once youth is gone it will never come back. So cherish your time and don't waste your youth.

画虎画皮难画骨，知人知面不知心

huà hǔ huà pí nán huà gǔ, zhī rén zhī miàn bù zhī xīn

In drawing a tiger, you show its skin, but not its bones; in knowing a man, you may know his face, but not his heart.

画一只老虎，容易画出它的皮毛却很难画出它的骨头；认识一个人，容易了解他的外表却很难了解到他的内心。

这条谚语告诉我们：了解一个人很不容易。特别是对那种表面一套、内心又是一套的人，应该处处提防，以免受骗上当。

This proverb points out that it is difficult to get to know what a person is really like.

面：面貌，表面。
Face.

火要空心, 人要虚心

huǒ yào kōngxīn, rén yào xūxīn

A fire must have space at its center to burn vigorously; a man must be modest to make progress.

　　火需要空心(柴火架空烧),才能燃烧旺盛;人应该虚心,才能不断进步。

　　这条谚语告诉我们:一个人要感到自己有很多不足的地方,随时随地学习新的东西,才能不断提高自己。

This proverb urges us to be aware of our deficiencies and improve ourselves all the time if we want to make progress.

见怪不怪，其怪自败

jiàn guài bù guài, qí guài zì bài

Face odd things fearlessly and their fearsomeness will disappear.

　　遇见怪异的事物，不奇怪，不惊恐，怪异的事物也就自行败退了。

　　这条谚语告诉我们：怪异的事物都有它自身发展和消失的规律。见到那些怪异的现象，不必大惊小怪，不必理睬它，随它而去好了。

This proverb tells us that alarming things have a way of developing and then dispersing. So, when faced with queer things, don't pay too much attention to them, as they will disappear by themselves.

败：失败，也可作消除、解除。

To fail; to dispel.

江山易改，本性难移

jiāngshān yì gǎi, běnxìng nán yí

Rivers and mountains may be changed, but it is hard to alter even a single person's nature.

　　江河山川的面貌容易改变，一个人的性格、习性却很难改变。

　　这条谚语告诉我们：一个人多年养成的作风、性情、习惯等很不容易在短时期内改变过来。

This proverb tells us that a person's temperament and habits developed over many years can hardly be changed in a short period of time.

本性:本来的性格、习性。
　　One's inherent quality.
移:改变。
　　To change, alter.

近水楼台先得月，向阳花木早逢春

jìn shuǐ lóutái xiān dé yuè, xiàngyáng huāmù zǎo féng chūn

A waterfront pavilion gets the moonlight first; spring comes early to plants exposed to the sun.

靠近水边的楼台最先得到水中的月影，向着太阳的花草树木最早焕发勃勃生机，所以长得茂盛。

这条谚语告诉我们：办成一件事情，需要依赖于一定的客观条件。条件方便的、优越的，往往成功较快；条件较差的，往往成功较慢，甚至不能成功。

This proverb points out that favorable conditions lead to rapid success, and vice versa.

春：这里比喻为生机。

Here referring to vitality and life.

近水知鱼性，近山识鸟音

jìn shuǐ zhī yú xìng, jìn shān shí niǎo yīn

Near to rivers, we recognize fish; near to mountains, we recognize the songs of birds.

接近江河才能知道鱼的特性，靠近山林才能识别鸟的鸣声。

这条谚语告诉我们：要想熟悉一个地方或一个人的情况，必须与这个地方或这个人经常接触。说明进行实地调查研究十分重要。

This proverb explains that, to become familiar with a place or a person, one has to keep in contact with it; it is very important to make on-the-spot investigations.

近朱者赤，近墨者黑

jìn zhū zhě chì, jìn mò zhě hēi

Near vermilion, one gets stained pink; near ink, one gets stained black.

经常靠近红色的东西,就会变成红的;经常靠近黑色的东西就会变成黑的。朱和赤都表示红色。

这条谚语告诉我们:经常接近好人就容易变好,经常接近坏人就容易变坏。强调社会环境(特别是朋友、亲属等关系密切的人)对一个人的影响。

This proverb tells us that one who associates with good people will learn to be good, while one who associates with bad people will learn to be bad. One is greatly influenced by one's close relationships and surroundings.

近:接近,靠近。
　　To be closed to.
朱、赤:都表示红色。
　　朱 and 赤 are both shades of red.
墨:用来代表黑色的东西。
　　Ink, referring to the color black.

酒逢知己千杯少，话不投机半句多

jiǔ féng zhījǐ qiān bēi shǎo, huà bù tóujī bàn jù duō

If you drink with a bosom friend, a thousand cups are not enough; if you argue with someone, half a sentence is too much.

　　遇见知心朋友,喝了千杯酒也感到太少;碰到谈不来的人,说上半句 话也觉得太多。

　　这条谚语告诉我们:人与人之间,相互理解和相互沟通是非常重要的。

This proverb tells us that mutual understanding is very important in human relationships.

知己:彼此相互了解而情谊深切的朋友。
　　Bosom friend.
投机:见解相同,很谈得来。
　　Congenial, agreeable.

老当益壮，穷当益坚

lǎo dāng yì zhuàng, qióng dāng yì jiān

Old but vigorous, poor but ambitious.

人老了，更应该充满干劲；人穷了，更应该坚强有志气。

这条谚语告诉我们：越是在困难的条件下，越应该有发奋的精神和顽强的毅力，不能被各种困难吓倒。

This proverb encourages us to pluck up courage when confronted with difficulties and never to be daunted.

当：应当。
　Should.
益：更加。
　More.

良药苦口利于病，忠言逆耳利于行

liángyào kǔkǒu lìyú bìng,　zhōngyán nì´ěr lìyú xíng

It takes bitter medicine to cure a disease properly, and it takes blunt advice to put us on the right track.

好药虽然味苦,却有利于治病;忠诚的劝告虽然听起来不顺耳,却有利于人的行为。

这条谚语告诉我们:真诚的批评、劝告,即使言词非常尖锐,却能帮助你改正缺点和错误,对你只有好处没有坏处。

This proverb stresses that honest advice and candid criticism, despite being unwelcome, are what we need if we are to identify our shortcomings.

良:好。
　　Good, fine.
忠言:诚恳劝告的话。
　　Honest advice.
逆(nì)耳:不顺耳,听起来感到不舒服。
　　Unpleasant to the ear.

两虎相斗，必有一伤

liǎng hǔ xiāng dòu, bì yǒu yī shāng

When two tigers fight, one is sure to lose.

　　两只老虎打架,必定有一只要受伤。

　　这条谚语告诉我们:双方争斗,总有一方要受到损害。劝戒人们不要盲目地互相争斗,盲目争斗的结果,只有害处,没有好处。

This proverb warns us that conflict between two sides results in one of them getting hurt. So it is best to avoid fighting as much as possible.

斗(dòu):争斗,打架。
　　To fight, struggle.

留得青山在，不怕没柴烧

liú dé qīngshān zài, bù pà méi chái shāo

As long as the green hills remain, there'll be no shortage of firewood.

只要青山存在，就不怕没有柴火烧。

这条谚语告诉我们：只要保存一定的基本实力，就不怕没有发展前途，最后达到理想的目的。这条谚语多用来告诫人们应该注意身体，有了健康的身体才能够完成艰巨的工作。

This proverb reminds us that as long as one preserves one's integrity the final goal will surely be attained. The proverb is also often quoted to advise people to take care of their health, which is the basic condition for fulfilling their tasks.

路遥知马力，日久见人心

lù yáo zhī mǎlì, rì jiǔ jiàn rénxīn

As distance tests a horse's strength, so does time reveal a person's real character.

路途遥远才能知道马的力量的强弱，相处时间长了才能看出人心的好坏。

这条谚语告诉我们：要想了解一个人思想、品质的好坏，能力的大小，只有通过长时间的考验。

This proverb tells us that a long period of testing is needed to understand one's nature and capabilities.

麻雀虽小，肝胆俱全

máquè suī xiǎo, gāndǎn jù quán

Small as it is, the sparrow has all the vital organs.

麻雀的身体虽然很小，但是它的五脏六腑是齐全的。

这条谚语告诉我们：尽管某种事物很小，但是包含的内容却样样齐全。也说明小事物同样会有代表性、典型性。

This proverb reminds us that something may be small in size, yet it may still contain all the necessary parts. The meaning is that something small may represent things much bigger and general.

俱:全,都。

　　All.

马好不在鞍，人好不在衫

mǎ hǎo bù zài ān, rén hǎo bù zài shān

Don't judge a horse by its saddle, and don't judge a person by his clothes.

一匹马是不是好,不在乎它的鞍子怎样;一个人是不是好,不在乎他穿的衣衫怎样。

这条谚语告诉我们:对待事物或评价一个人,不能光看表面,而要着重看他的实质。

This proverb tells us not to judge a person or thing simply by outward appearances.

明人不用细说，响鼓不用重捶

míng rén bù yòng xì shuō, xiǎng gǔ bù yòng zhòng chuí

A person of good sense needs no detailed explanation; a resonant drum needs no heavy beating.

聪明的人不需要详细的解说，响亮的鼓不需要重重地敲打。

这条谚语告诉我们：对于明白事情或精通某项专业的人，只需稍微点一下，他们就全懂了。不必花费过多的语言。说话要看对象。

This proverb reminds us people of good sense or expertise need only a hint to understand any matter. One has to consider one's audience when speaking.

捶：用棒槌敲打。

To beat with a stick.

明知山有虎，偏向虎山行

míng zhī shān yǒu hǔ, piān xiàng hǔshān xíng

Going deep into the mountains, undeterred by the tigers there.

明明知道山上有老虎，却偏要向有老虎的山上走去。

这条谚语有两种意思。第一种是：越是困难和艰险的地方，越是要去。表现了无所畏惧的精神。（含褒义）第二种是：明明知道前面有危险，却偏要冒险去干。（含贬义）

This proverb has two meanings: The more difficult and dangerous the place is, the more one wants to go there. It indicates a spirit of fearing nothing. Or it can mean that one knows well the dangers but insists on taking the risk anyway.

宁为玉碎，不为瓦全

nìng wéi yù suì，bù wéi wǎ quán

Better to be a shard of jade than a whole tile.

宁愿做一块玉而被打碎，不愿做一片瓦而得到保全。

这条谚语告诉我们：应该做一个为正义的事业而献身的英雄、勇士，而不应该做一个丧失人格、气节而保全性命的胆小鬼。

This proverb is a metaphor extolling the virtue of dying for a noble cause rather than living a shameful life.

宁：宁可，宁愿。

Would rather.

为：作为。

To be.

玉：比喻有价值的东西。

Jade, something valuable.

瓦：比喻没有价值的东西。

Tile, something worthless.

贫居闹市无人问，富在深山有远亲

pín jū nàoshì wú rén wèn, fù zài shēnshān yǒu yuǎn qīn

If you are poor, even if you live in a crowded city you will be alone. But if you are rich, even if you live in uninhabited mountains the most distant relatives will flock to you.

贫穷时，即使居住在热闹的都市也没有人来过问；富贵时，哪怕是住在深山里也有远房亲戚找上门来。

这条谚语反映了社会上某些人与人之间单纯金钱关系的不正常现象：亲与不亲完全决定于钱财的多和少。这种现象是应该改变的。

This proverb laments the fact that relationships among people too often depend on money.

平生不做亏心事，半夜敲门心不惊

píngshēng bù zuò kuīxīn shì, bànyè qiāomén xīn bù jīng

A clear conscience sleeps even through thunder.

一辈子不做对不起良心的事，半夜里听到敲门声心里也不会惊慌。

这条谚语告诉我们：平时为人诚恳正直，从来不做损人利己的事，那么无论什么时候都心安理得，不必担心有人上门来找麻烦。

This proverb is a reminder that so long as one never harms others, there is no need to fear any attack on one's integrity.

平时不烧香，临时抱佛脚

píngshí bù shāoxiāng, línshí bào fó jiǎo

Never burning incense when all is well, but clasping Buddha's feet in an emergency.

平时不去庙里给佛烧香磕头，遇到紧急事情才抱住佛的脚请求保佑已经来不及了。

这条谚语告诉我们：如果平常不事先做好准备，事到临头才慌忙想办法，（比如平时不用心学习，临到考试才慌忙应付）已经晚了。

This proverb warns us to take precautions against all emergencies, and not wait for disaster to strike.

千军易得，一将难求

qiān jūn yì dé, yī jiàng nán qiú

It is easy to find a thousand soldiers, but hard to find a good general.

上千人的军队很容易得到，一个好的将帅却很难寻求到。

这条谚语告诉我们：杰出优秀的将领或领导人才并不多，要找到这样的人才很不容易。

This proverb notes the difficulty of finding an outstanding leader.

钱财如粪土，仁义值千金

qiáncái rú fèntǔ, rényì zhí qiān jīn

Riches are as worthless as dust; benevolence and justice are the most valuable things.

金钱和财物像粪土一样没有什么价值，仁爱和正义比钱财更可贵。

这条谚语告诉我们：过去把仁爱和正义作为一个人为人的最高标准。和仁义相比，钱财是微不足道的东西。一个人切不可以为了钱财而抛弃了仁义。

This proverb stresses that benevolence and justice are the most valuable possessions. Compared with these qualities, wealth is worthless, and one should never discard benevolence for the sake of money.

前人栽树，后人乘凉

qiánrén zāi shù, hòurén chéngliáng

One generation plants the trees under whose shade another generation rests.

前辈人种植栽培了树木，后来的人就能在大树荫下乘凉。

这条谚语告诉我们：前辈人艰苦创业，是为了后代人生活幸福。后代人不可忘记前辈人的功劳。

This proverb tells us that we should never forget that the benefits we enjoy are the result of previous generation's hard work.

乘凉：热天在凉快的地方休息。

To rest in a cool place on a hot day.

强中更有强中手，能人背后有能人

qiáng zhōng gèng yǒu qiáng zhōng shǒu, néngrén
bèihòu yǒu néngrén

**However strong you are, there's always someone
stronger.**

强者当中还有更强的人，能人后面还有能力更大的人。

这条谚语告诉我们：做人一定要谦虚谨慎，切不可狂妄自大，因为在你的周围总会有本领和能力超过你的人。

This proverb advises us to be modest and prudent no matter how talented we are, because there is always someone better than we are at something.

强：优秀，能力强。

　　Excellent, capable.

能人：能力强、很有本事的人。

　　Capable man.

人过留名，雁过留声

rén guò liú míng, yàn guò liú shēng

A man leaves his name behind wherever he stays, just as a goose utters its cry wherever it flies.

人在哪里呆过，就会在那里留下名声，雁在哪里飞过，就会在哪里留下鸣声。

这条谚语告诉我们：人在哪里工作或生活过，总会在那里留下自己的名声。做了好事就留下好名声，干了坏事就留下坏名声。一个人应该珍惜自己的好名声。

This proverb reminds us that a person leaves a reputation, bad or good, behind wherever he works or stays. So one should try to make sure one preserves a good reputation.

名：名声。
Fame.

人老心不老，人穷志不穷

rén lǎo xīn bù lǎo, rén qióng zhì bù qióng

Old but young at heart;   poor but with lofty ideals.

人虽老了雄心并不衰退，人虽穷了志气不能消失。这里第二个"老"指衰退，第二个"穷"指消失。

这条谚语告诉我们：一个人不管在什么不利的情况下都应该保持远大的理想，保持雄心壮志。

The second 老 means decline; the second 穷 means vanish. This proverb advises us to have lofty ambitions and be unyielding in spirit in any unfavorable circumstances whatsoever.

人善被人欺，马善被人骑

rén shàn bèi rén qī, mǎ shàn bèi rén qí

A weak person is liable to be bullied; a tamed horse is often ridden.

温顺老实的人容易被人欺侮，温顺老实的马常常被人骑坐。

这条谚语告诉我们：过分老实是一个缺点。对待坏人切不能表现出老实、软弱，不然会受到欺凌。

This proverb warns that weakness is a disadvantage. Especially when confronting evil, a person must be tough, otherwise he will be bullied.

善：温顺老实。
Obedient and weak.

人往高处走，水往低处流

rén wǎng gāochù zǒu, shuǐ wǎng dīchù liú

Man seeks the heights, while water seeks the lowlands.

人朝着高的地方走上去，水朝着低的地方流下来。

这条谚语告诉我们：要不断进取，勇于向上攀登，干出一番事业。

This proverb encourages us to follow our natural inclinations to achieve success.

人为财死, 鸟为食亡

rén wèi cái sǐ,　niǎo wèi shí wáng

Man dies in pursuit of wealth, and birds die in pursuit of food.

人常常为了谋取钱财而丧失生命，鸟往往为了吃到食物而遭致死亡。

这条谚语告诉我们：不要过分地追求钱财。过分贪财的人，厄 (è) 运总有一天会降临到自己头上。

This proverb warns us against reckless pursuit of wealth. Ruin will befall the greedy sooner or later.

人无千日好，花无百日红

rén wú qiān rì hǎo, huā wú bǎi rì hóng

Man cannot be always fortunate, nor can flowers last forever.

人不可能长时间走好运，花儿不可能长时间红艳艳。千日和百日都形容时间很长。

这条谚语告诉我们：人生的道路不可能总是顺利的，总会遇到一些挫折和不幸。对此我们应该有正确的认识，在遇到挫折的时候，不要悲观失望。

Both 千日 and 百日 mean a long time. This proverb counsels that one is sure to meet setbacks and misfortunes in life; what is important is that one should face setbacks with a realistic attitude.

好：顺利,走运。
Smooth and lucky.

人无完人，金无足赤

rén wú wánrén, jīn wú zúchì

It is as impossible to find a perfect man as it is to find 100 percent pure gold.

人里面没有完美无缺的人，金子里面没有十足的纯金。

这条谚语告诉我们：人不可能没有一点缺点或错误，不能要求一个人十全十美，只要能够发扬优点，克服缺点就很好了。

This proverb cautions us that it is foolish to demand perfection. What we should do is concentrate on developing our merits and overcoming our shortcomings.

足赤:成色十足的金子。
　　100 percent pure gold.
赤:纯金。
　　Referring to pure gold.

人无远虑，必有近忧

rén wú yuǎn lǜ, bì yǒu jìn yōu

Those who do not plan for the future will find trouble on their doorstep.

一个人如果没有长远的考虑，就一定会有近期的忧患。

这条谚语告诉我们：平时要有长远的计划和安排，才不会出现近期的忧愁和烦恼。

This proverb advises us to make long-term plans in order to avoid troubles in the near future.

虑：考虑。
　Consideration.
忧：忧愁，忧患。
　Trouble, worry.

人心齐，泰山移

rénxīn qí, Tài Shān yí

When people are of one mind and heart, they can move Mount Tai.

假如人的心一致了，泰山也能移走。

这条谚语告诉我们：只要大家团结一致，齐心合力，就会力量无比，什么困难都能克服，什么事情都能办到。

This proverb advises us that as long as we unite as one, we will be strong enough to do anything and overcome any difficulties.

齐：　一致。

　　　Unity.

移：　移动。

　　　To move.

泰山：是中国山东省内的一座有名的高山，常用来代表很高的山。

　　　A famous mountain in Shandong Province, which was the highest mountain known to Confucius. It symbolizes a towering peak.

人有失足，马有失蹄

rén yǒu shī zú, mǎ yǒu shī tí

A man is prone to stumble when walking, and a horse is prone to stumble when galloping.

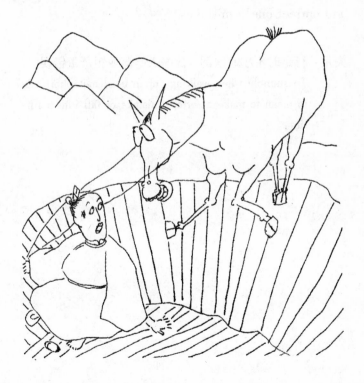

　　人走路时难免有脚没踩稳而摔跤，马在奔跑时难免有蹄子踏空而跌倒。

　　这条谚语说明任何一个人都难免有失误或犯错误的时候。重要的是有了错误应该认识和改正。

This proverb tells us that one can't avoid making mistakes; what is important is to recognize and correct one's mistakes.

失足：行走时不小心跌倒。比喻人堕落或犯严重错误。
　　To stumble when walking, often used metaphorically to mean to make a serious mistake or fall into perdition.

任凭风浪起，稳坐钓鱼船

rènpíng fēnglàng qǐ, wěn zuò diàoyú chuán

Sit tight in the fishing boat despite the rising wind and waves.

不管风有多大浪有多高，仍然稳稳当当地坐在钓鱼船上。

这条谚语告诉我们：面对复杂、险恶的情况，需要沉着镇定，毫不惊慌、动摇，才能转危为安，取得胜利。

This proverb explains that, when confronted with a complicated and perilous situation, it is best to be calm and unshaken.

任凭：无论、不管。
　　In spite of.

若要人不知，除非己莫为

ruò yào rén bù zhī, chúfēi jǐ mò wéi

If you don't want people to find out, you'd better not do it.

若要想让别人不知道,除非自己不去干。(多指干坏事)

这条谚语告诉我们:做了坏事是隐瞒不住的,迟早总会被人发现。

This proverb points out that wrongdoing will be revealed, sooner or later.

莫为:不去做。
　　Don't do.

三个臭皮匠，顶个诸葛亮

sān gè chòu píjiàng, dǐng gè Zhūgě Liàng

Three cobblers with their wits combined equal Zhuge Liang, the master mind.

三个补鞋子的皮匠凑在一起，智谋能赶得上一个诸葛亮。诸葛亮是三国时代蜀国的丞相，足智多谋。

这条谚语告诉我们：人多智慧多，办法多，计谋多。

This proverb calls our attention to the wisdom which resides in ordinary people.

诸葛亮： 三国时代蜀国的丞相，著名政治家和战略家。

A famous statesman and strategist, the prime minister of the State of Shu during the Three Kingdoms Period (220-280).

臭皮匠： 过去把皮匠一类职业的人看得很低贱，所以有这样的说法。

Cobbling was considered a very humble occupation.

顶： 赶得上，相当。

To match, equal.

三人一条心，黄土变成金

sān rén yī tiáo xīn, huángtǔ biànchéng jīn

If people are of one heart, even the yellow earth can become gold.

如果大家都是一个心眼儿，黄土都可以变成金子。黄土变成金是一种比喻。

这条谚语告诉我们：只要人们齐心协力，就能办好事情。

This proverb tells us that as long as people are unified, any goal can be achieved.

一条心：意思是一个心眼儿，心思一样。

Of one heart.

少壮不努力，老大徒伤悲

shàozhuàng bù nǔlì, lǎodà tú shāngbēi

A man who does not exert himself in his youth will be sorry he didn't when he grows old.

年轻力壮的时候不努力干出一番事业，年纪老了再悲伤后悔已经没有用了。

这条谚语告诉我们：不要虚度年华。趁年轻的时候抓紧学习，努力工作，干出一番事业，到老了才不至于感到后悔。

This proverb points out that if a person fritters away his youth in idleness, he will regret it when he grows old, but by then it will be too late.

徒：徒然；白白地；毫无用处地。

In vain.

十年窗下无人问，一举成名天下知

shí nián chuāng xià wú rén wèn, yī jǔ chéngmíng tiānxià zhī

One can study for ten years in obscurity, but as soon as one passes the examination the whole world pays attention.

在寒窗下苦读十年，没人理睬；一旦考中了，则闻名天下，身价百倍。

这条谚语是说：在过去的科举时代，读书人只有靠苦读诗书，考取功名，才能够出人头地。

This proverb encourages us to persevere despite the fact that no one seems to take any notice, for fame awaits at the culmination of a long period of toil.

十年树木，百年树人

shí nián shù mù, bǎi nián shù rén

It takes ten years to grow a tree, but a hundred years to bring up a generation of good men.

十年时间才能培植出树木，百年时间才能培养出人才。

这条谚语告诉我们：培养人才是一项十分艰巨的任务，需要做长期而耐心的工作。

This proverb means that cultivating talent is hard work which needs long and patient effort.

十、百：这里泛指多，不一定是实数。

　　十 and 百 here indicate a large number, not necessarily a definite number.

树：这里作动词，是种植、培育的意思。

　　Here as a verb, it means to plant or to ultivate.

书到用时方恨少

shū dào yòng shí fāng hèn shǎo

It is when you are using what you have learned from books that you wish you had read more.

读书到了要用的时候才悔恨读得太少。

这条谚语告诉我们：读书不多，到应用的时候就会感到知识不足。所以应该多读书，多积累知识。

This proverb reminds us that we can never read widely enough.

方：才。

Only, just when.

天外有天，人上有人

tiān wài yǒu tiān, rén shàng yǒu rén

As capable as you are, there is always someone more capable--just as there is another heaven beyond heaven.

天的外面会有更高的天，能人的上边会有能力更强的人。

这条谚语告诉我们：无论在哪一方面，比自己能力强的人总是有的，切不可骄傲自满，以为自己了不起，应该处处谦虚谨慎。

This proverb reminds us that there is always someone more capable than we are. So one should remain modest and prudent, and never become arrogant or conceited.

天下无难事，只怕有心人

tiānxià wú nán shì, zhǐ pà yǒuxīn rén

Nothing in the world is difficult for one who sets his mind to it.

世界上没有什么难办到的事情，只要有决心就总能成功。

这条谚语告诉我们：困难并不可怕，有决心和恒心的人，再困难的事情也不在话下。

This proverb tells us that a person with resolution and perseverance can solve the most difficult problem.

天下：天的下面，泛指世界。
　"Under Heaven", referring to the world.

天下兴亡，匹夫有责

tiānxià xīng wáng, pǐfū yǒu zé

Everyone is responsible for his country.

国家的兴盛或衰亡，每一个普通人都有责任来管。

这条谚语告诉我们：国家是众人的国家。每一个公民，应该关心国家的命运，为国家的命运负起责任。

This proverb stresses that every citizen has the responsibility for caring about state affairs and is responsible for the ups and downs of the country.

天下：多指国家。
　　"Under Heaven", meaning the nation.
匹夫：泛指平常人。
　　The common people.

天有不测风云，人有旦夕祸福

tiān yǒu bùcè fēngyún, rén yǒu dànxī huòfú

In nature there are unexpected storms, and in life unpredictable vicissitudes.

　　天上的风云变幻 (huàn) 难以预测，人的灾祸或者幸福一早一晚都可能降临。

　　这条谚语告诉我们：人的灾祸或幸福就像天上的风云那样难以预料。不必为暂时的祸患而苦恼悲伤，也不必为一时的幸福而得意忘形。

This proverb instructs that human disasters and fortunes are as unpredictable as the clouds and winds. Hence, don't worry about temporary calamities, nor be complacent about temporary joys.

旦夕：早晨和晚上，比喻短时间。
　　Morning and evening, indicating a short time.

万事俱备,只欠东风

wàn shì jù bèi, zhǐ qiàn dōngfēng

Everything is ready except the east wind.

中国古代的三国时代,吴国和蜀国联合,在赤壁抵抗魏国曹操大军的进攻。吴国周瑜定计用火焚烧曹操的战船。但是那时正当冬季,多刮西北风,而周瑜的舰队处于长江下游,在东面,曹操处于上游,在西面。进攻的各种准备工作都已做好了,只能等得蜀国足智多谋的诸葛亮借来东风,才能放火烧船。

这条谚语借用上面的故事,比喻各种条件都已经具备,只差最后一个关键性的条件,事情就能办成功了。

In the Three Kingdoms Period (220-280), the allied forces of the Kingdoms of Wu and Shu withstood an attack by the Kingdom of Wei's army led by the famous strategist Cao Cao. Zhou Yu of the Kingdom of Wu schemed to send fire ships to burn Cao Cao's fleet. But it was winter at that time, and Zhou Yu's fleet was in the east on the lower reaches of the Yangtze River, while Cao Cao's fleet was in the west, on the upper reaches. Everything was ready for the attack except for an east wind, needed to blow the fire ships toward Cao Cao's fleet. This proverb, derived from the above story, means that everything is ready except what is crucial.

俱:都,全。All, everything.

小洞不补, 大洞叫苦

xiǎo dòng bù bǔ,　dà dòng jiào kǔ

A small hole not mended in time will become a big hole much more difficult to mend.

小洞如果不把它补好，变成大洞就难补了，就要叫苦了。

这条谚语告诉我们：小问题如果不及时处理好，发展成为大的问题就难于解决了。

This proverb tells us that if a trivial problem is not solved in time, it will become a serious and knotty one.

小时偷针，大时偷金

xiǎo shí tōu zhēn, dà shí tōu jīn

A child who steals a needle will grow up to steal gold.

小的时候偷了别人的针，长大以后就可能去偷别人的金钱。

这条谚语告诉我们：对孩子小时候的坏习惯，比如小偷小摸要引起重视，抓紧教育，否则将来就可能发展成为犯罪行为。

This proverb directs our attention to the importance of correcting the bad habits of children, no matter how trivial. Otherwise, the bad habits may develop into serious criminal behavior. By then it will be too late.

心正不怕影斜，脚正不怕鞋歪

xīn zhèng bù pà yǐng xié, jiǎo zhèng bù pà xié wāi

An upright man is not afraid of an oblique shadow; a straight foot is not afraid of a crooked shoe.

心底正直就不怕影子是斜的，脚跟站稳就不怕鞋子是歪的。

这条谚语告诉我们：心地磊落的人不怕人散布流言蜚 (fēi) 语；行为正直忠实的人不怕别人歪曲诬陷。

This proverb tells us that an upright man fears no gossip or slander.

秀才不出门，能知天下事

xiùcai bù chū mén, néng zhī tiānxià shì

Without even stepping outside his gate the scholar knows all the wide world's affairs.

秀才不必走出家门，就能够知道世界上的许多事情。

这条谚语告诉我们：书本是知识的宝库。人只要多读书，即使没有外出，也能从书本上获得许多有用的知识。

This proverb reminds us that books are treasure-houses of knowledge. If one reads a lot, he can learn a great deal of useful knowledge without bothering to seek it in the wide world.

秀才：中国明朝和清朝时候，通过最低一级考试合格的读书人。后来用来泛指有学问的读书人。

One who passed the imperial examination at the county level in the Ming and Qing dynasties. Later it came to be used to refer to scholars in general.

养兵千日，用在一时

yǎng bīng qiān rì, yòng zài yī shí

Armies are to be maintained in the course of long years, but to be used in the nick of time.

长时期地供养和操练军队，是为了一旦需要时立刻投入战斗。

这条谚语告诉我们：经过长时期的训练和准备，才能应付一时紧急的需要。说明平时训练和准备十分重要。

This proverb shows that training and preparation in normal times will enable one to cope with emergencies.

千日：指很长时间。
　　A long time.
一时：指短时间。
　　A short time.

一寸光阴一寸金, 寸金难买寸光阴

yī cùn guāngyīn yī cùn jīn, cùn jīn nán mǎi cùn guāngyīn

A speck of time is more precious than an ounce of gold.

一寸光阴等于一寸金子，一寸金子却难以买到一寸光阴。

这条谚语告诉我们：时间是一个非常宝贵的东西，时间流逝了，黄金也难以买回。应当珍惜你的时间啊!

This proverb tells us that time is the most precious thing in the world.

光阴:指时间。
　　Time.

一个篱笆三个桩,一个好汉三个帮

yī gè líba sān gè zhuāng, yī gè hǎohàn sān gè bāng

Just as a fence needs the support of three stakes, an able fellow needs the help of three other people.

围一个篱笆至少要打三个桩子，当一个英雄好汉少不了要三个帮手。

这条谚语告诉我们：要干出一番事业，需要发挥集体的力量，一个人不管他的本领有多大，也需要别人的帮助。

This proverb points out that to fulfil any task, the support of others is necessary. Regardless how capable one is, one still needs the help of others.

篱笆：用竹子或树枝等编成的围墙。

Fence made of bamboo or tree branches.

三个：表示多数。

三个 here indicates several.

好汉：勇敢坚强或者有作为的男子。

A stalwart man.

一粒老鼠屎，坏了一锅粥

yī lì lǎoshǔ shǐ, huàile yī guō zhōu

A speck of mouse dung will spoil a whole pot of porridge.

一粒老鼠屎掉进锅里,把一锅粥都搞坏了(一锅粥都不能吃了)。

这条谚语告诉我们:只要有一点点坏的或有害的东西,就会使一个整体遭到破坏。如个别人不良的思想行为,会影响到集体的形象。

This proverb points out that even a little bit of something bad or harmful will destroy the whole of the thing it touches. So, a bad man or a bad influence, if not curbed in time, will bring about catastrophe.

一年之计在于春，一日之计在于晨

yī nián zhī jì zàiyú chūn, yī rì zhī jì zàiyú chén

The whole year's work depends on good planning in spring, and the whole day's work depends on good planning in the early morning.

一年的计划要在春天安排好，一天的计划要在早晨安排好。

这条谚语告诉我们：做任何事情应该早有计划，早作安排，才能争取主动，取得成功。

This proverb tells us that good planning beforehand is the precondition for success.

计:计划。
Plan.

一人得道，鸡犬升天

yī rén dé dào, jī quǎn shēng tiān

When a man is at court, all his followers are in favor.

中国有个神话传说：有一个人修道成了仙，在他快要升天的时候，把修炼用的药喂了他的鸡和狗，鸡和狗也随着他升上了天。

这条谚语比喻：一个人有了权势，同他有关系的人也跟着沾光。

A fairy tale goes like this: A man who had attained the secret of immortality was about to ascend to Heaven. He fed his dogs and chickens with some of the elixir he had used. So the dogs and chickens went up to Heaven together with him.

This proverb is used metaphorically to mean that when a man rises in the world, all his friends and relations—even the most humble-benefit.

得道：指教徒学到了教义。

(Originally for a follower of Taoism) to attain the Way.

(Now) to be in power.

一失足成千古恨，再回头是百年身

yī shīzú chéng qiāngǔ hèn, zài huítóu shì bǎinián shēn

One single slip brings eternal regret, and looking back, you find that your whole life has passed away.

一次严重的错误，往往会造成永远的悔恨，想改正，却已经一辈子过去了。

这条谚语告诉我们：做人要十分谨慎。人的一生最多不过百年。如果犯一次严重错误，往往会悔恨终身。

This proverb cautions us to be careful of our behavior. One's lifetime can hardly be more than a hundred years; a serious mistake will easily result in a lifetime's regret.

失足：比喻人堕落或犯严重错误。
Making a serious mistake in life.
千古：长远的年代。
Eternal, for all time.
百年：人的一生时间，一辈子。
One's whole life.

一言既出，驷马难追

yī yán jì chū, sì mǎ nán zhuī

A word, once it is uttered, cannot be overtaken even by swift horses.

一句话已经说出口，哪怕是四匹快马同时去追，也追不回来。

这条谚语告诉我们：话已经说出了口，就无法再收回。因此，说话要慎重，说了之后，一定要守信用。

This proverb means that what is said cannot be unsaid. One must be careful what one says and be cautious about making promises.

言：话。
   Words.
既：已经。
   Already.
驷马:同拉一辆车的四匹马。
A team of four horses which draw a chariot.

一朝被蛇咬，十年怕草绳

yī zhāo bèi shé yǎo, shí nián pà cǎoshéng

A man once bitten by a snake will for ten years shy at a rope.

一旦被蛇咬了，许多年后看见草绳也感到害怕。

这条谚语告诉我们：一次不幸受到伤害，会产生一种恐惧心理，以后看见类似的东西也感到害怕。

This proverb wryly points out that we will be frightened of anything that looks like something which has once harmed us.

一朝：一天。

　　Some day.

十年：比喻时间很长。

　　(Here) a long time.

草绳：因它和蛇的样子相似，看到草绳容易联想到蛇。

　　Straw rope.

一着不慎，满盘皆输

yī zhāo bù shèn, mǎn pán jiē shū

One careless move forfeits the whole game.

一步关键的棋没有走好，就会使全盘棋都输掉。

这条谚语告诉我们：一个关键性的问题处理不当，就会使全局工作受到损失，以致完全失败。

This proverb warns us that if a crucial problem is not handled properly, the overall situation will be affected, finally leading to disaster.

一着：一步棋。

    One move in chess.

皆： 都。

    All.

有借有还，再借不难

yǒu jiè yǒu huán, zài jiè bù nán

Timely return of a loan makes it easier to borrow a second time.

借了别人的东西，如果能做到按时归还，下次再借就容易借到了。

这条谚语告诉我们：哪怕是借东西这种小事情，也要注意讲信誉守信用。

This proverb indicates that even in such a trivial matter as a loan, keeping one's word to the letter is necessary if one wants to have smooth dealings with others.

有理走遍天下，无理寸步难行

yǒulǐ zǒu biàn tiānxià, wúlǐ cùnbù nán xíng

**With justice on your side, you can go anywhere;
without it, you can't take a step.**

有道理走遍全世界都行得通，没道理很小的一步也难跨过去。

这条谚语告诉我们：掌握真理十分重要。有了真理，可以畅行无阻；没有真理只会处处碰壁。

This proverb stresses the fact that righteousness will see you through all difficulties, whereas without it your progress will be hampered from the very start.

有缘千里来相会，无缘对面不相逢

yǒuyuán qiānlǐ lái xiānghuì, wúyuán duìmiàn bù xiāngféng

Fate brings people together no matter how far apart they may be.

有了缘分，哪怕相隔千里也能聚会在一起；没有缘分，就是对面走过也不会见到。

这条谚语说明两个人的结合(如男女的恋爱、婚姻)或认识(如朋友、同事)都具有一定的缘分。

This proverb points out that human relationships are decreed by Fate.

缘：多指人与人之间注定要发生遇合的机会。

Fate, predestination.

与君一夕话，胜读十年书

yǔ jūn yī xī huà, shèng dú shí nián shū

Chatting with you for one night is more profitable than studying for ten years.

　　和对方一晚上的谈话，胜过自己读了十年的
书。

　　这条谚语夸张地说明对方一番谈话给自己的
印象深、教育大，收获超过了多年所读的书本知
识。

This proverb contains a high form of praise, to
the effect that one is deeply impressed and greatly
enlightened by someone else's conversation.

君：　对人的尊称。

　　　A respectful way to address a man.

夕：　晚上。

　　　Evening, night.

十年：多年的意思，不是实数。

　　　Many years　(not a definite number).

远水不救近火，远亲不如近邻

yuǎn shuǐ bù jiù jìn huǒ, yuǎn qīn bù rú jìn lín

Distant water can't put out a nearby fire, and a distant relative is not as helpful as a close neighbor.

处在很远的水,扑灭不了身边的大火;居住很远的亲戚,不如住在附近的邻居。

这条谚语告诉我们:比较遥远的美好设想,往往解决不了眼前急待解决的问题;关系再密切的亲戚不如附近的邻居能随时互相帮助。

This proverb tells us that a lofty ideal often cannot solve an urgent problem, just as a close relative who lives far away is not as valuable as a neighbor in an emergency.

月满则亏，水满则溢

yuè mǎn zé kuī, shuǐ mǎn zé yì

The moon waxes only to wane, and water surges only to overflow.

月亮圆了又要变成缺的，水太满了就要漫
(màn)出来。

这条谚语告诉我们：物极必反。也就是事物发
展到了极端，就会向相反的方向转化。

This proverb points out that: things turn into
their opposites when they reach their extremes.

亏：表示缺。

To wane.

溢：表示液体装得太满而漫出来。

To overflow.

在家不会迎宾客，出外方知少主人

zài jiā bù huì yíng bīnkè, chūwài fāng zhī shǎo zhǔrén

If a person does not treat guests properly when at home, few will wish to entertain him when he is away from home.

在家的时候不好好地接待客人，出门在外才知道接待自己的人太少了。

这条谚语告诉我们：人与人之间的关系是互相的。你热情诚恳地对待别人，别人也就会热情诚恳地对待你。

This proverb stresses that relations between people are reciprocal; others will treat you in the way you treat them.

知己知彼，百战百胜

zhī jǐ zhī bǐ, bǎi zhàn bǎi shèng

Know the enemy, know yourself, and in every battle you will be victorious.

知道自己的情况也知道对方的情况，哪怕一百次作战也能取得一百次胜利。

这条谚语告诉我们：既要了解自己，又要了解对方，发挥自己的长处，攻击对方的短处，这样才能有把握取得胜利。

This proverb advises: Know both yourself and your opponent in order to enhance your strong points and attack his weak points. That is the secret of victory.

彼：指对方（敌方）。

The other party (here: one's opponent).

只许州官放火，不许百姓点灯

zhǐ xǔ zhōuguān fànghuǒ, bù xǔ bǎixìng diǎndēng

The magistrates are free to set fires, while the common people are forbidden even to light lamps.

中国宋朝时有个名叫田登的人，做了州官。因为他的名字"登"和"灯"同音，所以不准百姓提到"点灯"的事。元宵节点彩灯时，田登发出布告说："本州依例放火三日。"用"放火"代替"放灯"。

根据以上故事引出这条谚语，用来讽刺有些统治者只许自己胡作非为，却不许别人拥有正当的言行和权利。

In the Song Dynasty a new magistrate called Tian Deng forbade the local people to say "light the lamp", because "lamp" (dēng) sounded like his name. When the Lantern Festival came around, a notice was posted: "With the permission of our magistrate, the people may set fires for three days." By "set fires" was meant "display lanterns". This proverb, derived from the above story, satirizes rulers who indulged in doing all kinds of evil things, but deprived the common people of their basic rights.

只要功夫深，铁杵磨成针

zhǐyào gōngfu shēn, tiěchǔ móchéng zhēn

If you work hard enough at it, you can grind even an iron rod down to a needle.

只要功夫到了家，哪怕是很粗的铁杵也能磨成细针。

这条谚语告诉我们：只要有决心，肯做长期不懈的努力，任何事情都能成功。

This proverb encourages us to persevere in whatever we undertake. Just as the English proverb has it: "Constant drilling can wear away a stone".

深：指时间长，也指本领高。

Long time; high skill.

杵(chǔ)：一头粗一头细的铁棒，用来捣碎粮食等。

A club used to pound grains.

种瓜得瓜，种豆得豆

zhòng guā dé guā, zhòng dòu dé dòu

As a man sows, so shall he reap.

种瓜就会得到瓜,种豆就会得到豆。

这条谚语告诉我们:做了什么样的事情,就会得到什么样的结果。做了善事,会得到好的报应;做了恶事,会得到坏的报应。事物间有一定的因果关系。

This proverb warns that one receives just returns for one's actions; good for good, and evil for evil.